DEDICATION

*To the memory of my mom,
Susan Mbi Enoh, a woman who
knew how to talk to God*

ACKNOWLEDGMENT

My gratitude to the Good Lord for believing in me and entrusting me with this work. A special thanks to Mary, Our Blessed Mother for her constant help. And to all my cheerleaders in heaven, I am grateful.

A special thanks to the priests at my local parishes, for their great teachings. A very big thanks to Ingrid Berganza for assisting with the Spanish translation of this book. To my editors, mentors, family and friends, I extend my gratitude.

And to my children, Michael and Raphael, thanks and let's never cease to pray.

Together, we will do great things!

FOREWORD

Prayer is the heart of Christian Spirituality. It is a relationship rather than a rule - a relationship with God, who is a Person and a loving Father. No one gets tired of beholding and speaking with a lover or a beloved.

Having a conversation with someone we love and someone we believe loves us increases our joy in good times, brings us consolation in sorrow, soothes our pain, adds to our courage when afraid, and ensures our peace in despair.

No wonder St. Paul enjoins us to "pray without ceasing" (1 Thessalonians 5:16). In other words, to continually draw closer to God. But how could this be achieved amidst the busy schedule of the day?

Dr. Elizabeth gives us a practical answer to this important question in this little book you just opened. In her usual way of expressing deep thoughts succinctly, she has formed simple and short prayers for almost all human endeavors: beginning from an unrecognized action of holding one's car key to something as simple and indiscernible as adding spices to food.

These pithy prayers are rooted in scripture and could serve as the popular traditional ejaculatory prayer or aspiration recommended by the Church. It could also be another way of knowing and gaining mastery of our Biblical texts by praying the Word of God.

You can be sure of one thing: that making them part of one's daily routine and memorizing them, if possible, saves us from the sloth and apathy to prayer, which could result from distractions from gadgets or being worn out from the enormous work of the day.

Fr. Matthew Nwafor

CONTENTS

Dedication————————————————————3
Acknowledgement——————————————4
Foreword——————————————————————5
Introduction—————————————————11
Holding Car Keys——————————————13
Putting On Shoes——————————————14
Turning On Lights——————————————15
Washing Your Hands————————————16
When Tired——————————————————17
Drinking Water————————————————18
Brushing Teeth————————————————19
Harvesting ——————————————————20
Driving——————————————————————21
Washing Dishes————————————————22
Doing Laundry————————————————23
Cooking—————————————————————24
Watching A Movie——————————————25
Incense In Church——————————————26
Insects——————————————————————27
Kneeling In Church——————————————28
Looking At Self In The Mirror————————29
Knocking At A Door——————————————30
Opening A Door————————————————31
Putting Gas In Car——————————————32

Upon Seeing Any Cross	33
Shutting Car trunk/door	34
Picking Up Mail	35
Taking A Walk	36
Unpacking Groceries	37
Taking Out Trash	38
Driving By Construction Site	39
Sweeping Floor	40
Taking A Shower	41
On The Phone	42
Going to bed	43
Waiting At A Traffic Light	44
Waiting At A Drive Through	45
Taking off Glasses	46
Carrying a Baby	47
Looking At Birds	48
Turning On Stove	49
Putting On Clothes	50
Serving Food	51
At Work	52
Walking Into A Dark Room	53
Putting On Name Tag	54
Walking With An Elderly	55
Plugging A Charger	56
Getting Up In The Morning	57
Making Up Bed	58
Holding A Pen	59

Putting Spices in Food-----------------------------------60
With Each Step---61
Under An Umbrella--------------------------------------62
Backing Up Car---63
Sharing Gifts---64
Itchy Head---65
Putting On Earrings-------------------------------------66
Fixing Hair---67
Beautiful Flower--68
Washing Face--69
At A Car Wash---70
Picking Up A Child-------------------------------------71
Carrying A Load---------------------------------------72
Dancing---73
The Sunrise---74
Cleaning A Sink---------------------------------------75
Going Through An Automated Car Wash-----------------76
Putting On Makeup------------------------------------77
Giving a Handshake-----------------------------------78
Looking At A Clock------------------------------------79
Folding Clothes---------------------------------------80
Walking by Green Trees-------------------------------81
Ironing Clothes---------------------------------------82
Hugging Someone-------------------------------------83
Watering Garden-------------------------------------84
Texting--85
Putting Bags Down-----------------------------------86

9

Sitting Down ---- 87
Laughing ---- 88
Vacuuming ---- 89
Turning On Headlights ---- 90
Taking Vitamin Tablets ---- 91
Procession At Church ---- 92
Carrying Water ---- 93
Looking At Watch ---- 94
Applying Lotion ---- 95
Deleting Old Text Messages ---- 96
Pruning Flowers ---- 97
Removing Weeds ---- 98
Starting Car ---- 99
Opening Wallet ---- 100
Heating Food In Microwave ---- 101
Leaning On A wall ---- 102
Putting Stuff In a Bag ---- 103
Spraying Airfreshner/Perfume ---- 104
Opening Blinds/Windows ---- 105
Climbing stairs ---- 106
Swimming ---- 107
Putting on Seat Belt ---- 108
Eating ---- 109
Putting Salt In Food ---- 110
Unwrapping A Candy ---- 111
The End ---- 112
Reference ---- 113

INTRODUCTION

Finally, a practical and simple guide to pray without ceasing is here. Prayer is communication with God. It may get overwhelming trying to catch up with the many prayers and devotions that are all good. I found myself in this difficult and sometimes confusing place, going from one prayer to another and one prayer line to another just to be able to connect with God.

It was at this junction that I was inspired to try to simplify things. This book is written in an effort to improve our prayer life. If you are a "Martha", preparing meals for others, or if you are a "Mary" just sitting at the feet of Jesus, this book is for you.

You do not have to be worried about not having time for prayers. This book encourages you to talk and listen to God as you go about your daily activities. Praying does not have to be a chore or a ritual in itself.

The prayers in this book are short and simple and have become part of my daily routines. I encourage you to make them your own as well.

Whether you are in the kitchen, you are encouraged to talk to God as you move the pots and pans. Or if you are a busy mom or dad, taking kids to soccer games etc, you are encouraged to pray your way through it all.

Do not wait until it is a perfect time, when everything is quiet to pray. Pray at all times.

When the mind is consumed with praying throughout the day, the evil one stays far away from you.

This book is easy and simple to read for everyone. The pictures make it even easier.

The good Lord is waiting to hear from you!

HOLDING CAR KEYS

Guide and direct me this day Lord, for you alone hold the key to my life, Amen. (John 3:16)

PUTTING ON SHOES

Guide my feet O Lord in the way of peace, Amen. (Luke 1:79)

TURNING ON LIGHTS

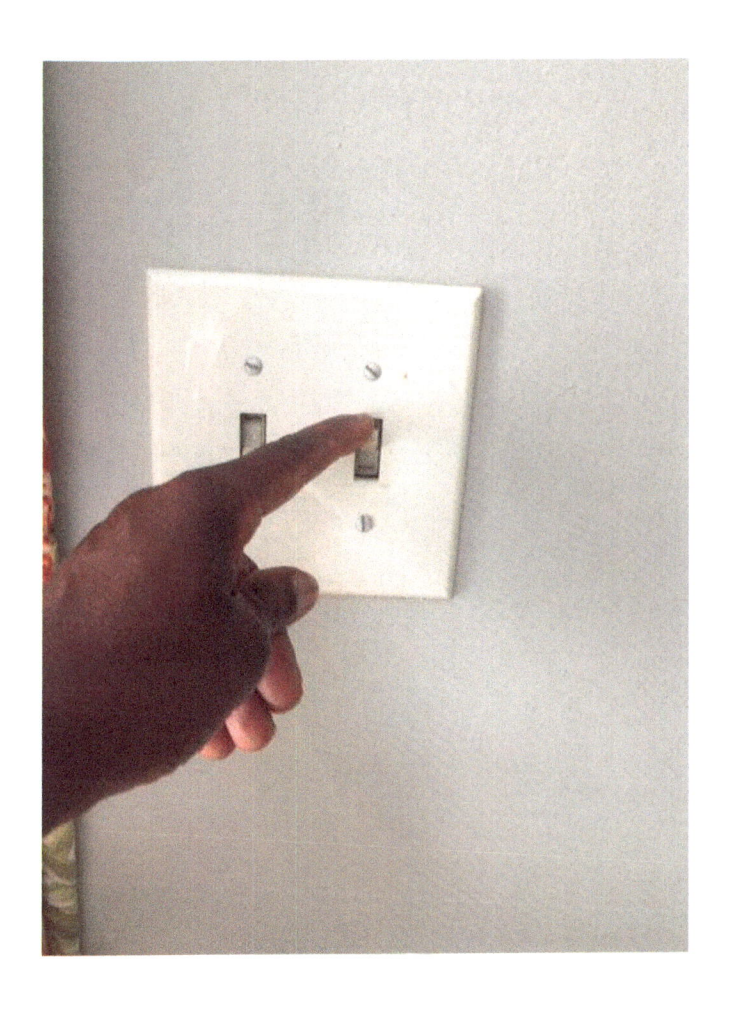

Lord, please let your light shine upon me(John 8:12)

WASHING HANDS

Lord, wash away all my iniquities, cleanse me from my sins, Amen.
(Psalm 51:2)

WHEN TIRED

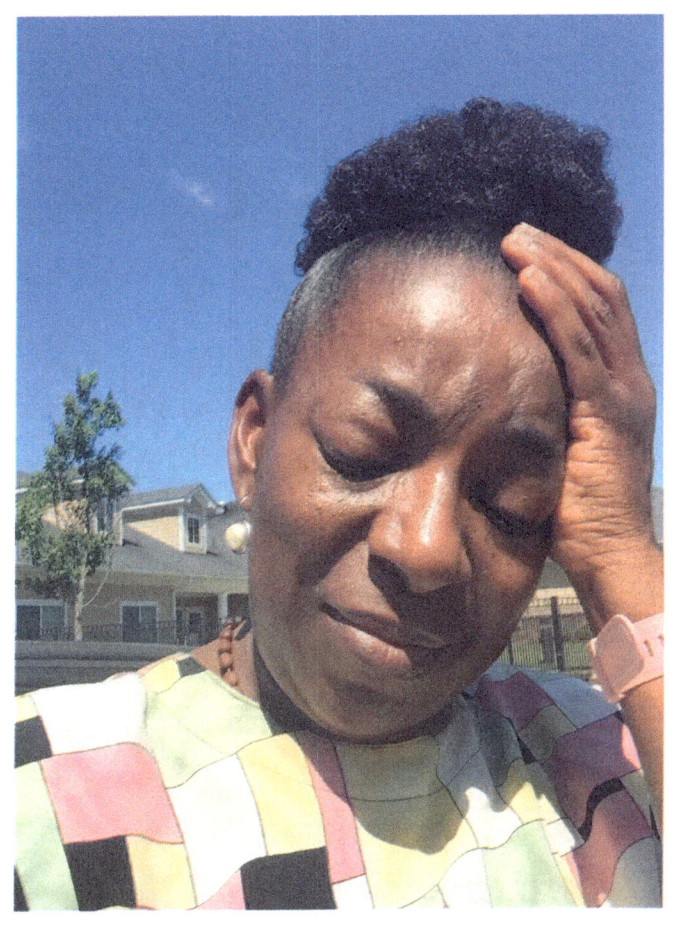

Strengthen me O, Lord for I am weak and tired, in Jesus name, Amen.
(Psalm 28:7)

DRINKING WATER

O Lord, please quench the thirst for you in my soul, in Jesus name, Amen. (Ps 42:3)

BRUSHING TEETH

Dear Lord, please let the words of my mouth be acceptable to you, in Jesus name, Amen. (Ps 19:14)

HARVEST FROM YOUR GARDEN

Dear Lord, please grant me patience, for I am confident that I will reap the fruits of my labor if I do not give up, Amen. (Ps 128:2)

DRIVING

Dear Lord, please lead me along the right paths as you have promised, Amen.
(Ps 23:3)

WASHING DISHES

Lord, wash me clean from any stain of sin, Amen.(Ps 51:7)

DOING LAUNDRY

Cleanse me O Lord from all unrighteousness, in Jesus name I pray, Amen.(1 Jn 1:9)

COOKING

Thank you Lord for always providing my daily bread, Amen.(Ps 23:1)

WATCHING A MOVIE

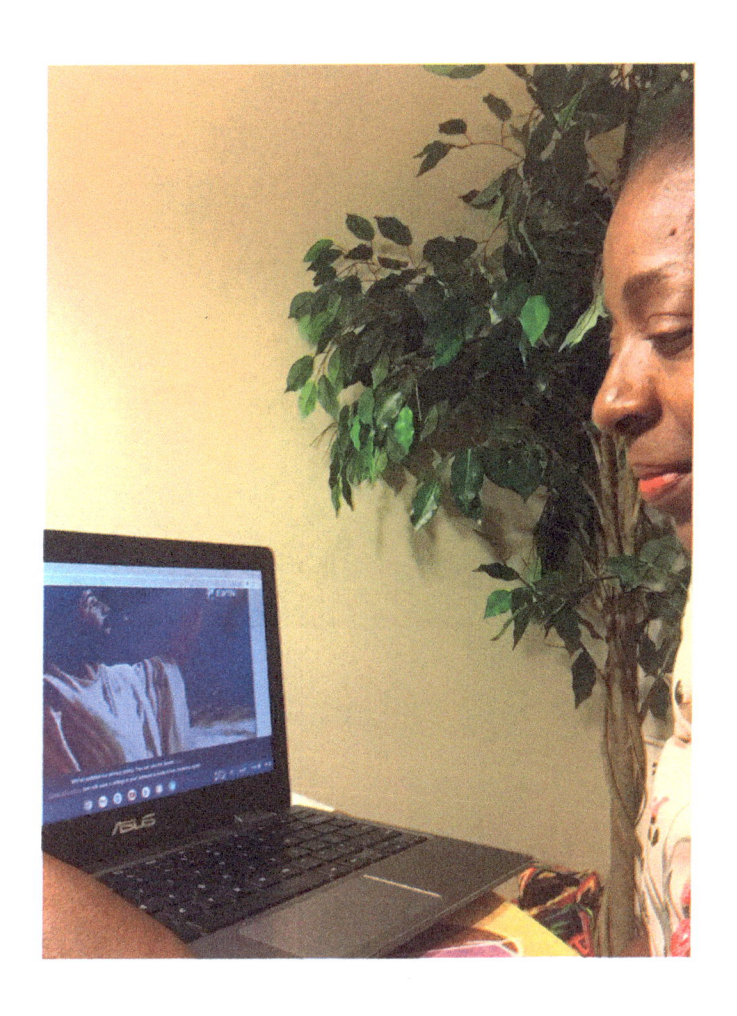

Thank you, dear Lord, for watching over me tirelessly, Amen. (Ps 121:5)

INCENSE IN CHURCH

Dear Lord, as the incense rises up so also may our prayers rise up to you, in Jesus name, Amen.(Mark 11:24)

INSECTS

Dear Lord, please keep far from us the evil one and his agents in Jesus name, Amen. (Jn 17:15)

KNEELING IN CHURCH

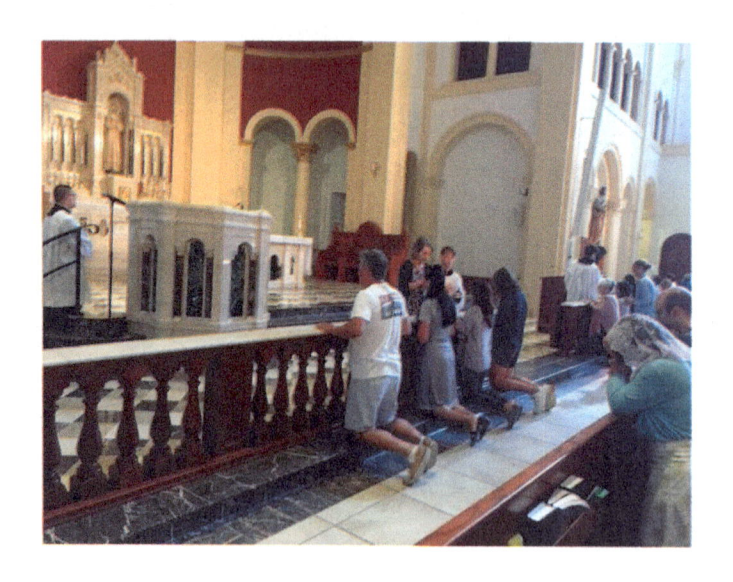

I kneel before you O Lord, Jesus Christ for at the mention of your name every must bow, Amen. (Phil 2:10)

LOOKING AT YOURSELF IN A MIRROR

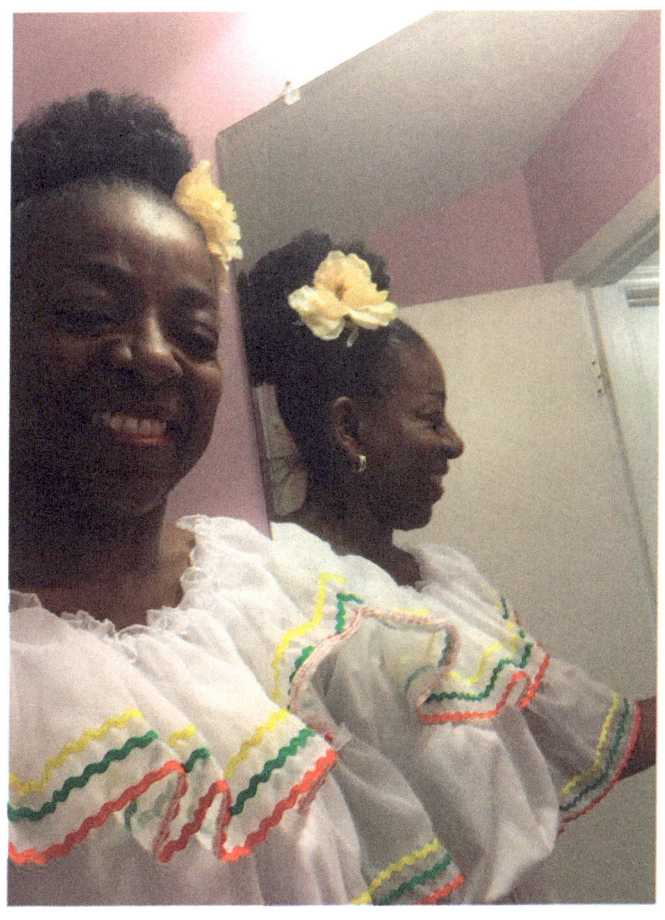

Thank you Lord for I am beautifully and wonderfully made, in Jesus name, Amen (Ps 139:14)

KNOCKING ON A DOOR

My God, please open the door when I knock as you have promised, Amen. (Matt 7:8)

OPENING A DOOR

My God, please come into my heart and grant me rest.(Matt 11: 28)

PUTTING GAS IN CAR

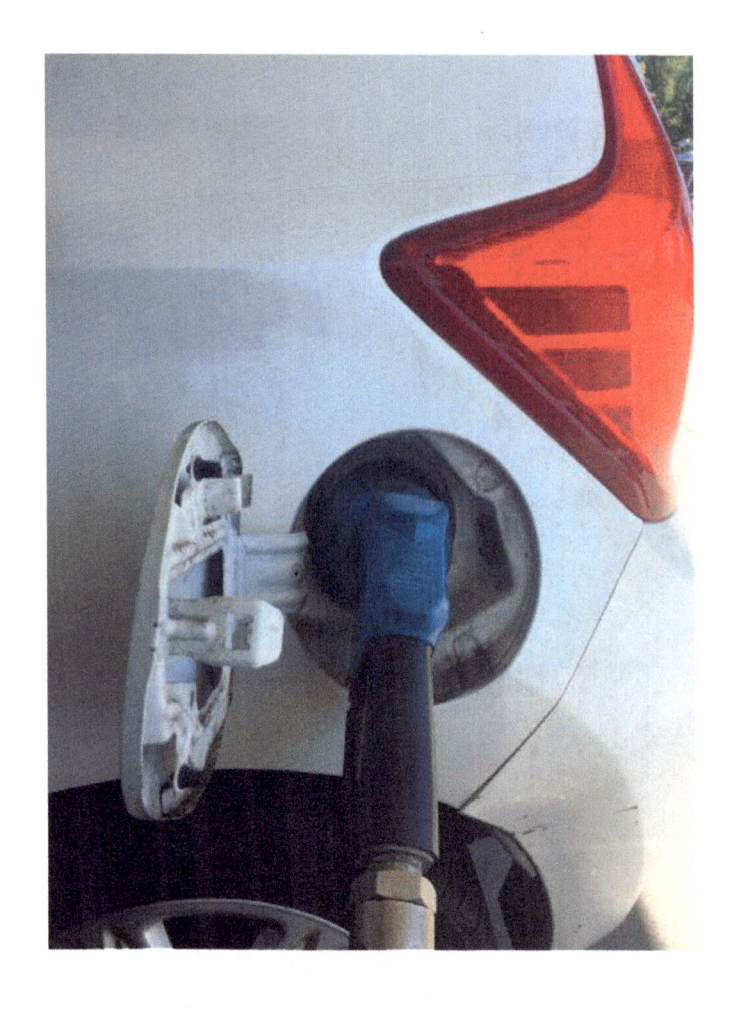

Fill me Lord with your constant love, in Jesus name, Amen.(Jer 31:3)

ON SEEING ANY CROSS

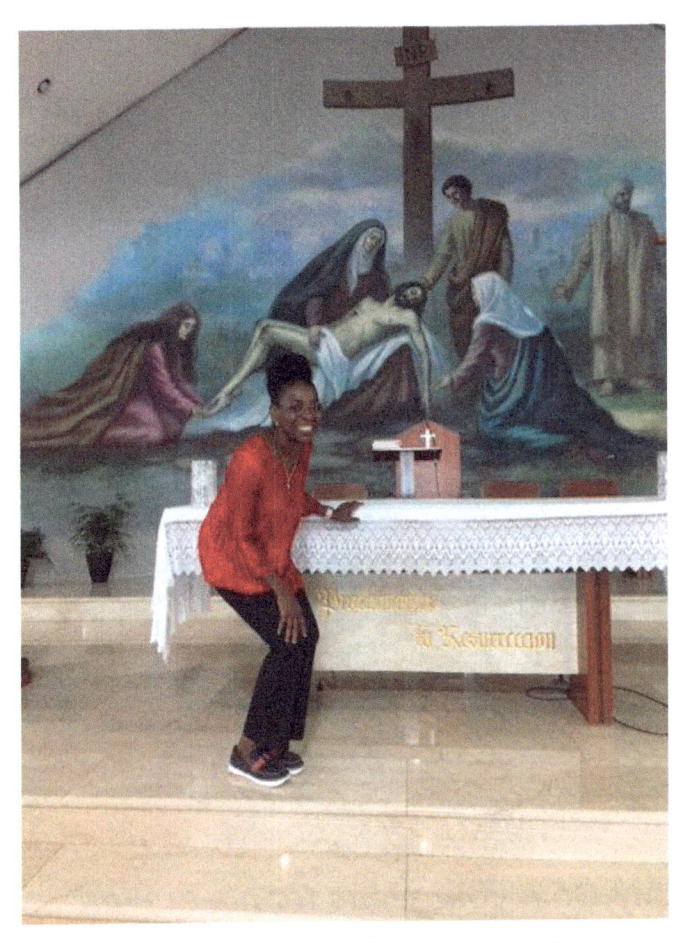

We adore you O Christ and we bless you, because by your Holy Cross You have redeemed the world. (1 Peter 2:24)

SHUTTING CAR TRUNK/DOOR

My God, your plans for me are for good and not for evil and I am confident that you have something better for me when you close a door, Amen. (Jer 29:11)

PICKING UP MAIL

My God, please grant me the grace to receive every gift, good or bad that you send to me with joy, in Jesus name, Amen. (Job 2:10)

TAKING A WALK

Lord, as I walk through this valley of the shadow of death, I will fear no evil, for you are always with me, Amen. (Ps 23:3)

UNPACKING GROCERIES

Thank you my Lord and Good Shepherd for providing all I need, in Jesus name, Amen
 (Ps 23:3)

TAKING OUT TRASH

My God, please take the trash out of my life and make me pure and Holy, in Jesus name, Amen.(1 Cor 5:7)

DRIVING BY A CONSTRUCTION SITE

My God, please grant me the patience to wait for the unfolding of your will just as the builders have to patiently wait for the completion of a new building, in Jesus name, Amen. (Ps 106:13)

SWEEPING THE FLOOR

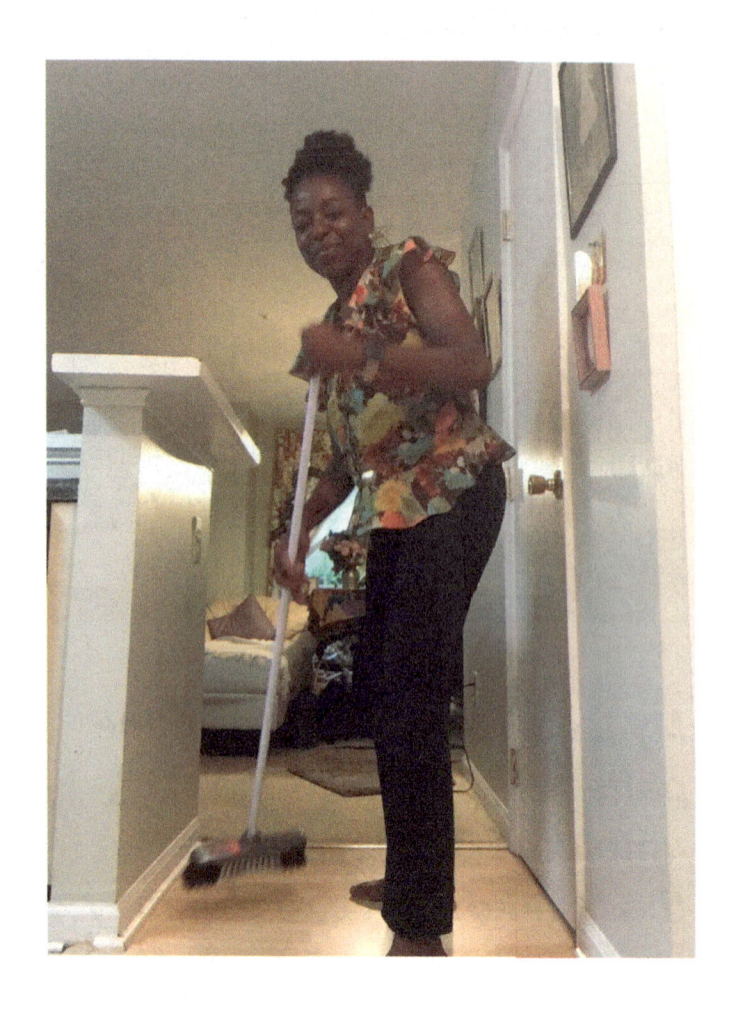

My God, kindly sweep away my offenses. Amen (Ps 50:3)

TAKING A SHOWER

My God, let your shower of blessings rain down upon me and my family, Amen.(2 Cor 9:8)

ON THE PHONE

My God, please do not delay, answer me when I call, Amen (Jer 33:3)

GOING TO SLEEP

I will both lay me down and sleep for you O God keep me in perfect peace. (Ps 4:8)

WAITING AT A TRAFFIC LIGHT

My God, help me to cling to the hope you give me in the hard moments of waiting.
(Rom 12:12)

WAITING AT A DRIVE THROUGH

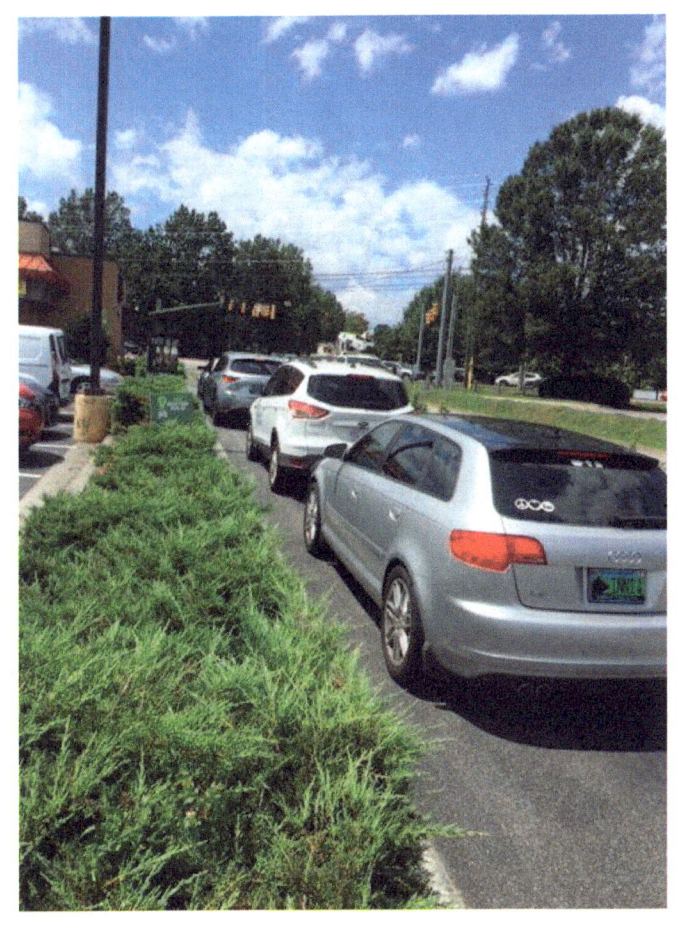

My God forgive my impatience and please give me the patience I need to wait with hope and joy, Amen.(Ps 40:1-2)

TAKING OFF GLASSES

My God, give me eyes to see what you are doing in my life. I pray for a heavenly perspective on my situation, not an earthly one, Amen. (Matt 13:16)

CARRYING A BABY

My God I thank you for caring for me. (1 Peter 4:7)

LOOKING AT BIRDS

My God who takes care of the birds will also take care of me, Amen. (Matt 6:26)

TURNING ON THE STOVE

My God, let the fire of your love burn in my heart. (Song of Songs 8:6)

PUTTING ON CLOTHES

O, Lord please clothe me with your joy and peace, Amen. (Col 3:12-15)

SERVING FOOD

I will serve you O Lord with gladness, Amen.(Ps 100:1-5)

AT WORK

My God, please help me to be amazing each day and find enjoyment in doing my work, Amen. (Eccl 2:24)

WALKING INTO A DARK ROOM

My God, I may be in the dark but you are my light and darkness cannot put you out, Amen.(John 8:12)

PUTTING ON NAME TAG

Yahweh Nissi, you are my banner, please grant me success at work today, in Jesus name, Amen.(Exodus 17:15)

WALKING WITH AN ELDERLY

My God, please walk me with every step of the way, Amen. (Matt 28:20)

PLUGGING A CHARGER

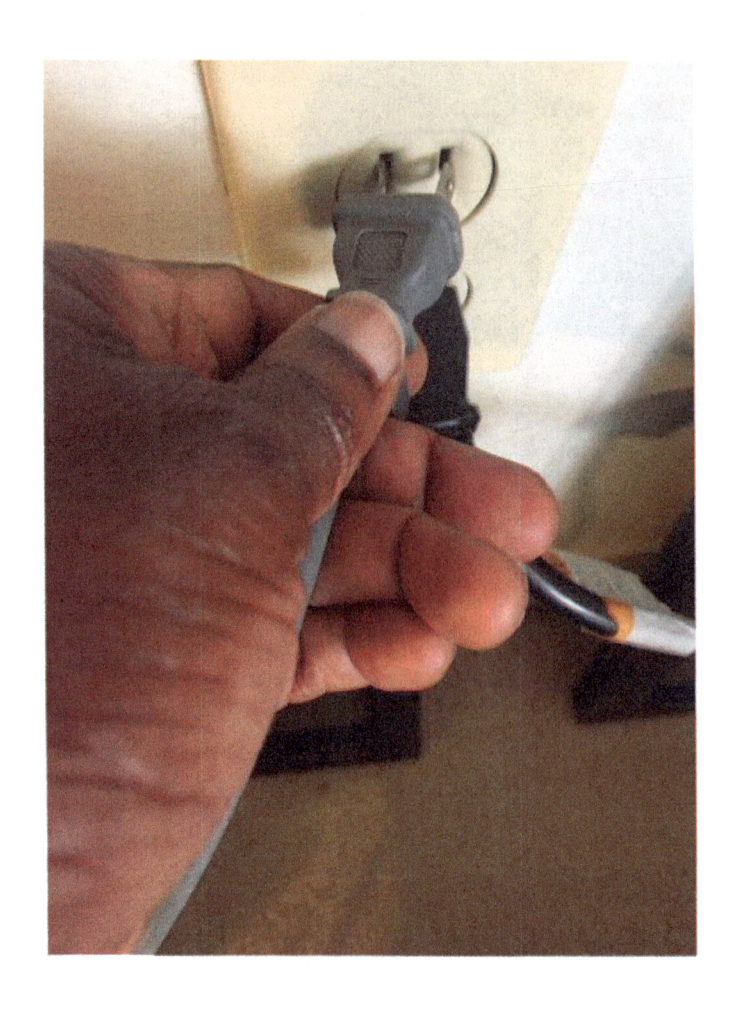

My God, deliver me from every distraction so as to stay connected to you, Amen. (John 15:4)

GETTING UP IN THE MORNING

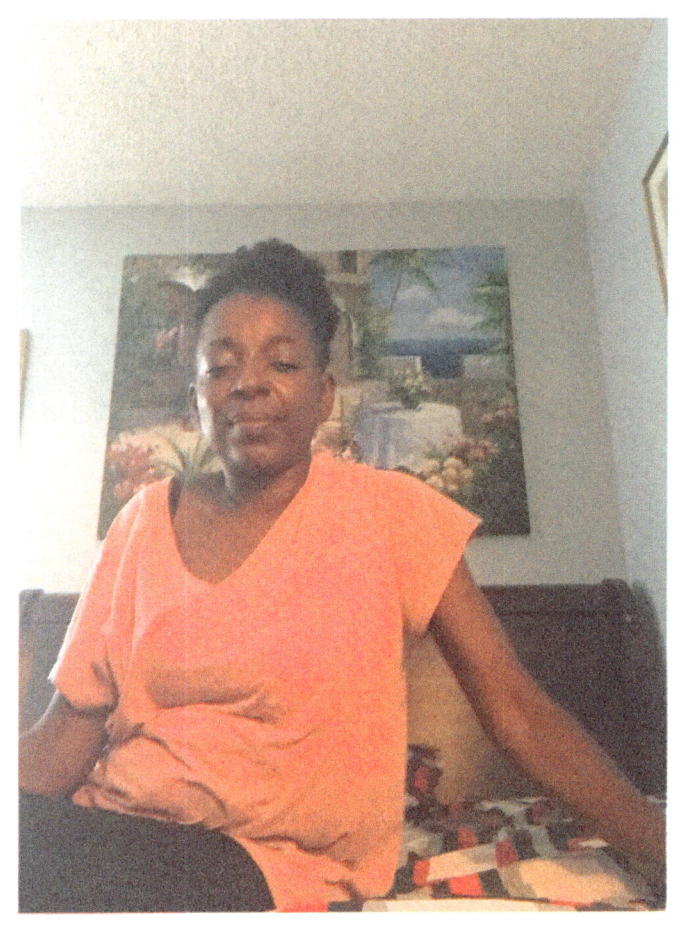

Thank you dear Lord for the gift of another new day, I will rejoice and be glad in it, Amen. (Psalm 118:24)

MAKING UP BED

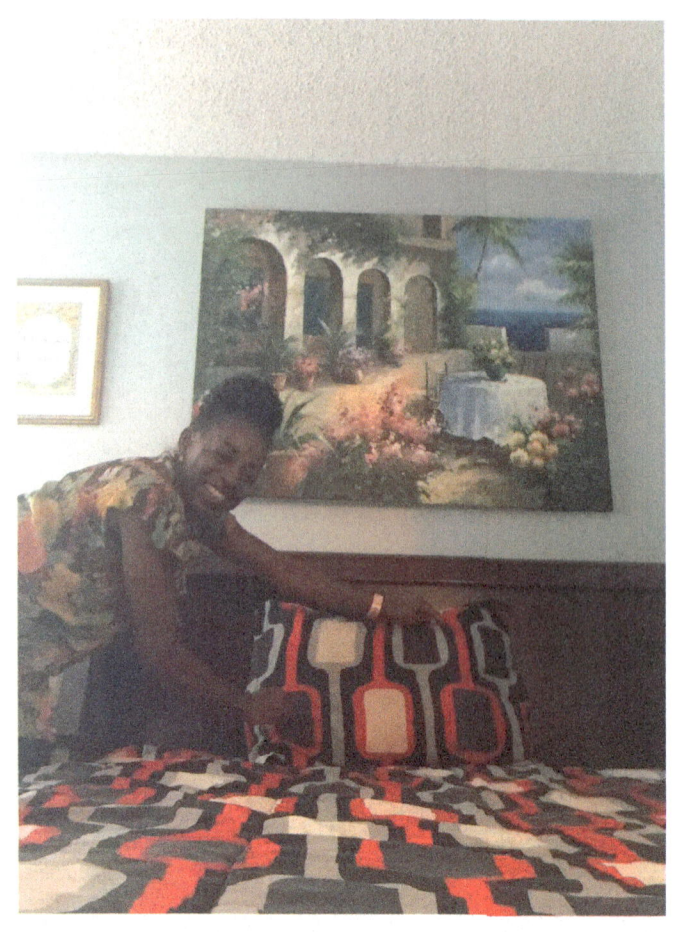

My God, help me to make my bed and to do all what you require of me this day very well, in Jesus name, Amen. (Prov 1:26-31)

HOLDING A PEN

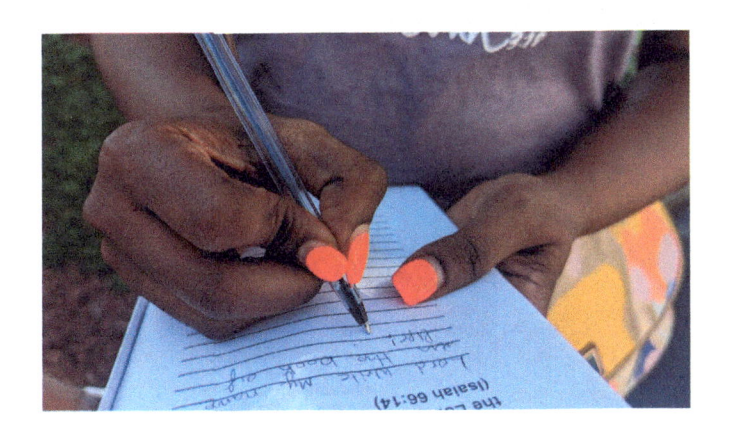

*My God, please write my name in your book of life, Amen.
(Rev 20:15)*

PUTTING SPICES IN FOOD

My God, just as these spices together make the food taste better than when used individually, I am confident that all things together will always work for my good (Rom 8:28)

WITH EACH STEP

My Lord, just as one leg goes forward before another, help me to take one day at a time, Amen.(Matt 6:25-34)

UNDER AN UMBRELLA

My God, I thank you for covering me under the safety of the shadow of your wings, Amen. (Ps 91:4)

BACKING UP CAR

The past will not be useful, for I am striving forward, forgetting those things which are behind and reaching forward to those things which are ahead of me in Jesus name, Amen. (Phil 3: 13-14)

SHARING GIFTS

Give me a generous heart O Lord, for I know that the measure I give, will be the measure I will receive, Amen.
(Luke 6:38)

ITCHY HEAD

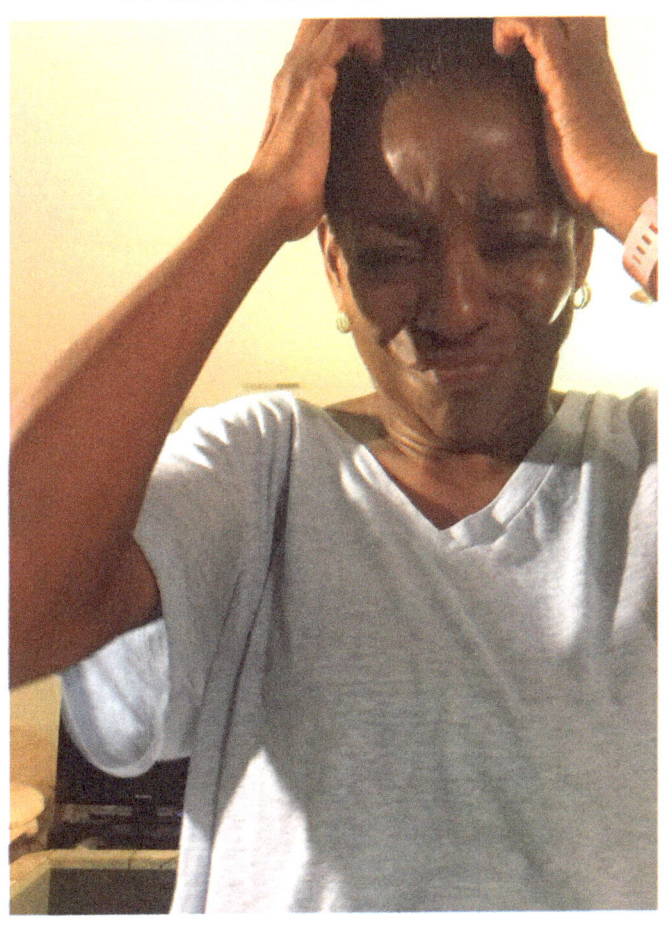

I will be anxious for nothing but with prayers and supplications with thanksgiving, make my requests known to the Lord, Amen. (Phil 4:6-7)

PUTTING ON EARRINGS

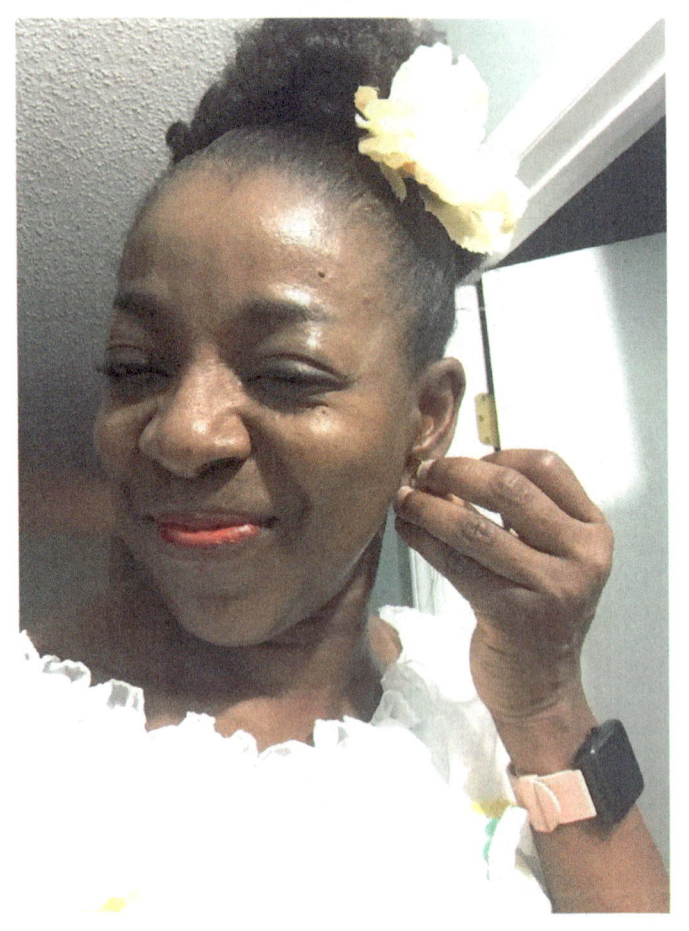

Speak Lord, for my ears are attentive to you, Amen.(1 Sam 3:7-11)

BEAUTIFUL FLOWER

The grass withers, the flower fades, but the word of God will stand forever, Amen. (Isaiah 40:8)

FIXING HAIR

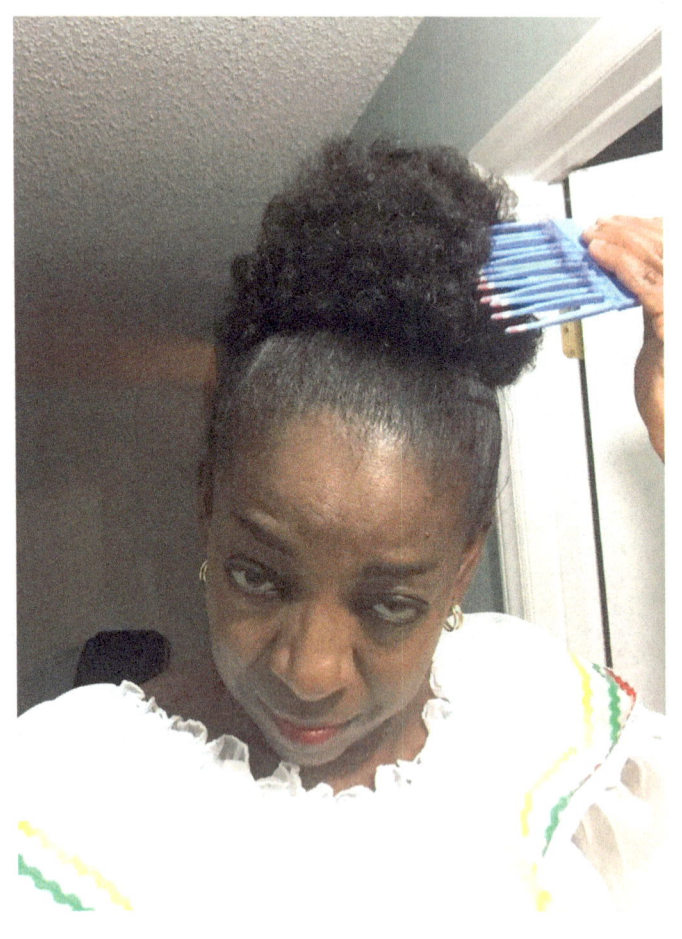

Thank you Lord, for taking very good care of me, Amen.
(1 Peter 5:7)

WASHING FACE

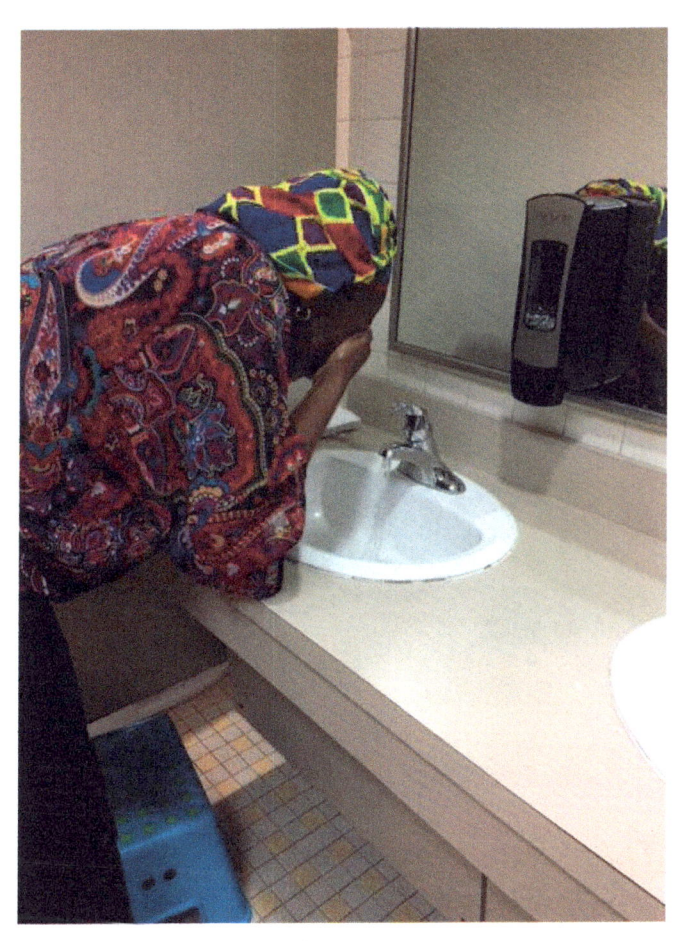

My God, do not hide your face from me, in Jesus name, Amen. (Ps 102:2)

AT A CAR WASH

Thank you Lord for your mercy, for I am confident that though my sins are as scarlet, they shall be as white as snow after you wash me up, Amen. (Isaiah 1:18)

PICKING UP A CHILD

I will extol thee, O Lord, for thou hast lifted me up and hast not made my foes to rejoice over me, Amen. (Ps 30:1)

CARRYING A LOAD

My God, please send me a "Veronica" and a "Simon of Cyrene" to help me carry my heavy load, in Jesus name, Amen.(Lk 23:26)

DANCING

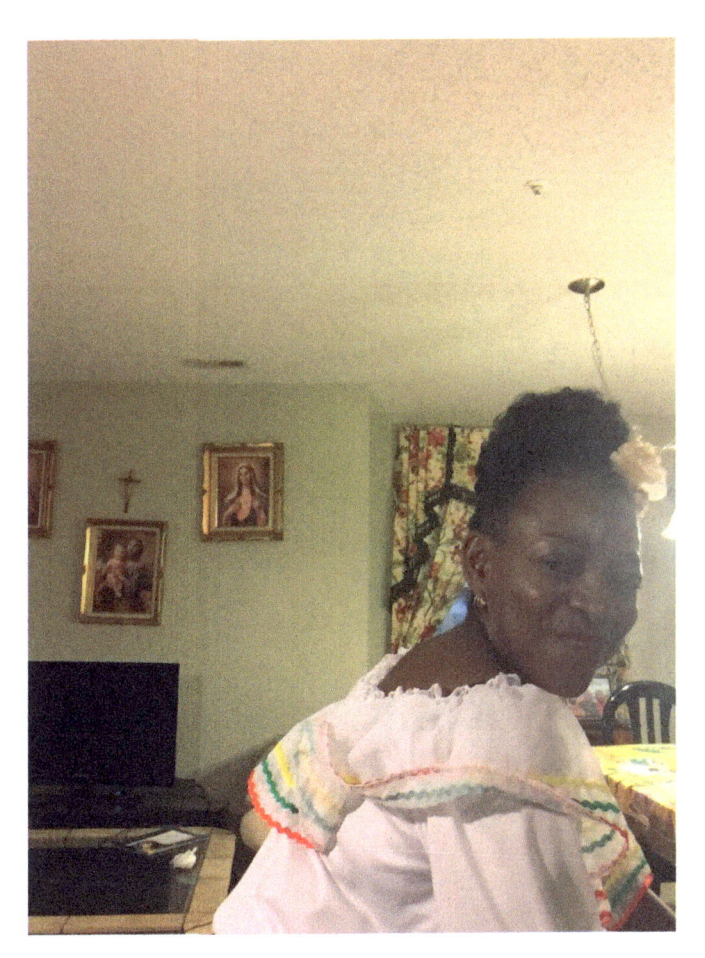

Those that sow in tears, shall reap rejoicing, Amen. (Ps 126:5-6)

THE SUNRISE

From the rising of the sun to its setting, may the name of the Lord be praised, Amen.
(Ps 113:3)

CLEANING SINK

My God, please cleanse and forgive my sins and grant me the grace to forgive others as well, in Jesus name, Amen. (Isaiah 1:18)

GOING THROUGH AN AUTOMATED CAR WASH

Just as I trust that this automatic machine will move me forward, dear Lord please augment my trust in you, Amen.(Matt 17:20-21)

PUTTING ON MAKEUP

My God, you make all things beautiful in your time, Amen.(Eccl 3:11)

GIVING A HANDSHAKE

Thank you Lord for the gift of one another, Amen.(Rom 12:5)

LOOKING AT A CLOCK

My God, please give me patience to wait for your perfect timing, Amen. (2 Peter 3:8)

FOLDING CLOTHES

My God, I thank you for clothing me, Amen. (Lk 12:27)

WALKING BY GREEN TREES

Planted in the house of the Lord, my leaves shall be evergreen and I shall flourish and yield fruit even in old age, Amen. (Ps 92:13-15)

IRONING CLOTHES

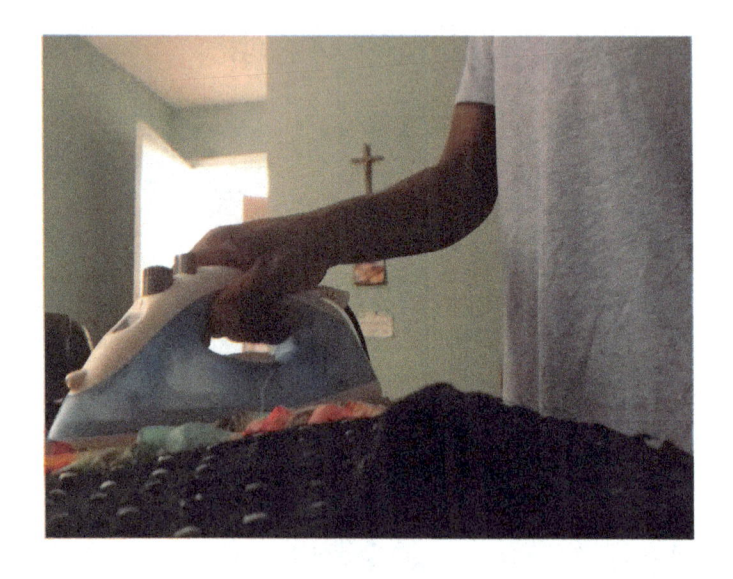

My God, when the intense pressure of that hot iron is removing the wrinkles from my heart, give me strength to endure, Amen. (Matt 24:13)

HUGGING SOMEONE

I am convinced that nothing in all creation will be able to separate us from the love of God that is in Christ Jesus, Amen. (Rom 8:38-39)

WATERING GARDEN

My God please pour down your blessings upon my family I have planted and watered, but you O Lord, give the increase, through Christ our Lord, Amen(1 Cor 3:6-8)

TEXTING

My God, may I use my fingers to bless and not to condemn anyone in Jesus name, Amen. (Matt 7:1)

PUTTING DOWN BAGS

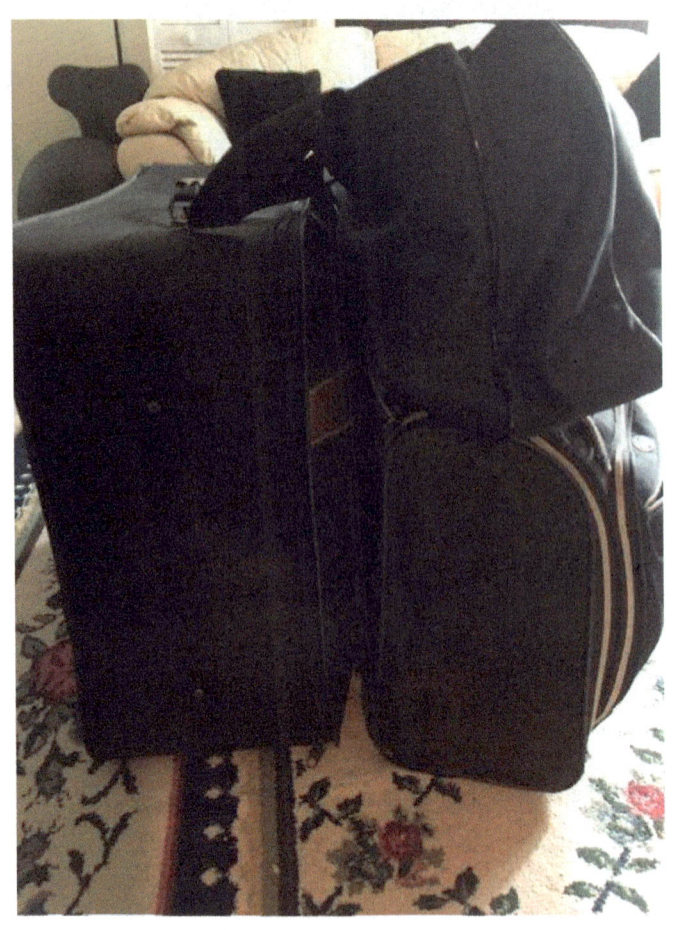

My God, I lay my burdens on you alone, for I know that you care for me, Amen. (1 Peter 5:7-10)

SITTING DOWN

Be still and know that I am God.(Psalm 46:10)

LAUGHING

My God, I thank you for the gift of laughter, please help us to laugh together so as to add fuel to each other's flame, Amen. (Prov 17:22)

VACUUMING

Create in me O Lord a clean heart in Jesus name, Amen.(Psalm 51:10-12)

TURNING ON HEADLIGHTS

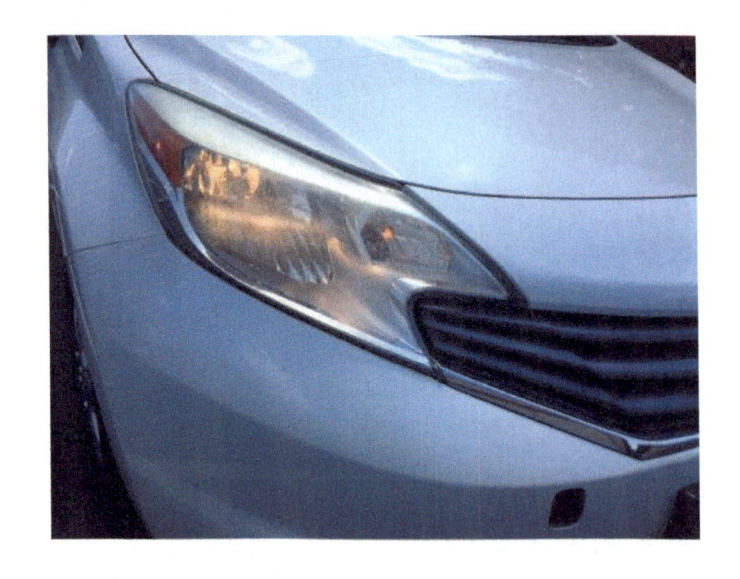

My God, with you, in you and through you, I will arise and shine this day in Jesus name, Amen. (Isaiah 60:1)

TAKING VITAMIN TABLETS

Just as I take my daily vitamins for the functioning of my body, may I never forget my daily dose of your word of life, Amen. (Heb 4:12)

PROCESSION AT CHURCH

When the saints go marching, Lord I want to be in the number, Amen.(1 Thessa 4:16)

CARRYING WATER

With joy I will fetch water from the wells of salvation (Isaiah 12:3)

LOOKING AT WATCH

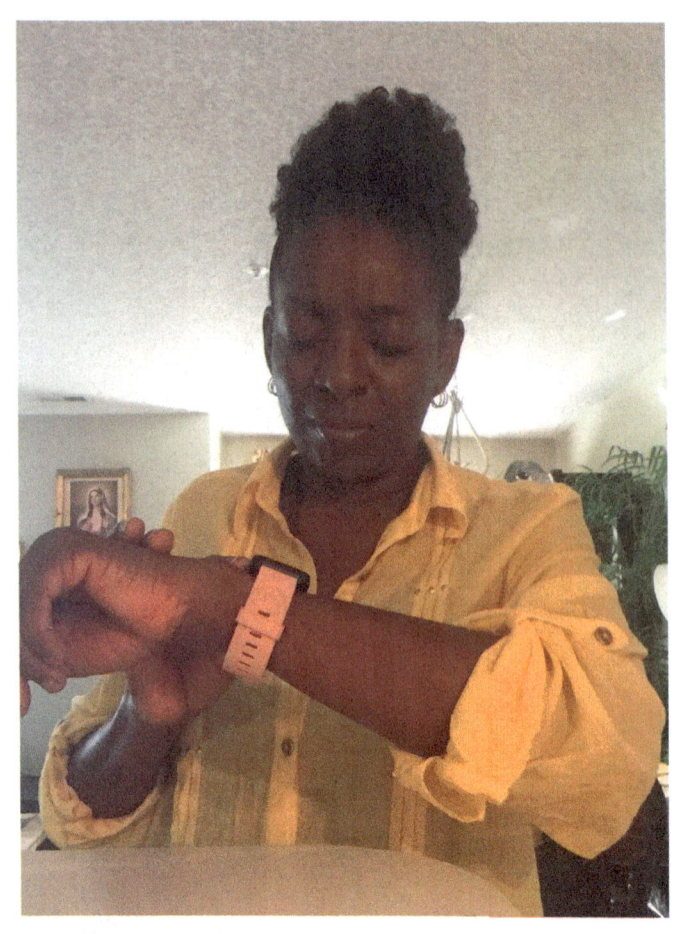

My God, it is never too late for you, for the things that are impossible with men are possible with you, Amen(Lk 18:27)

APPLYING LOTION

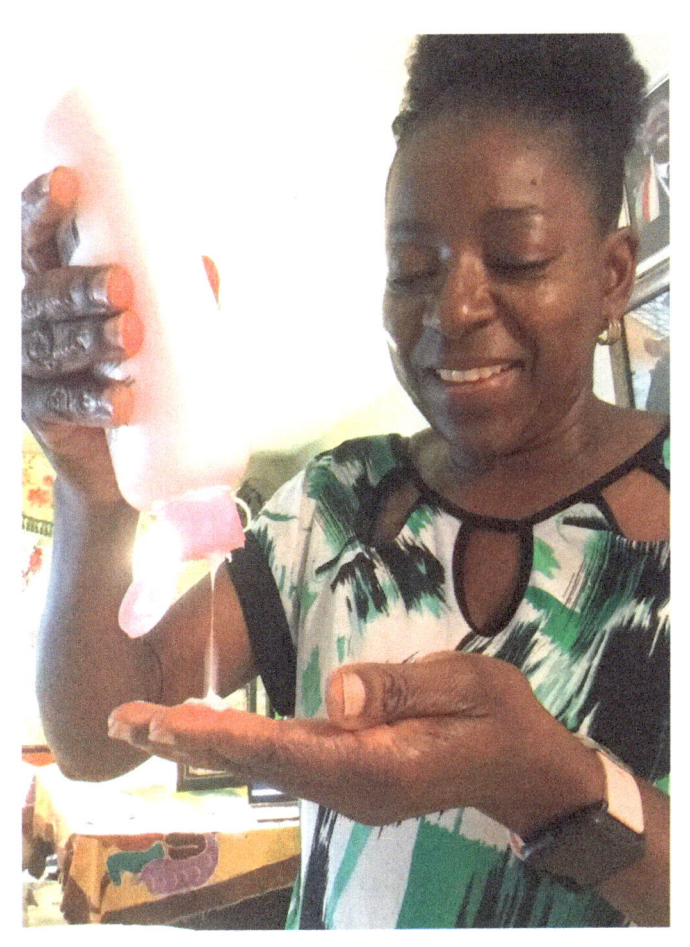

Anoint me Lord, with your spirit of love, peace and joy, Amen.(1 Sam 16:13)

DELETING TEXT MESSAGES

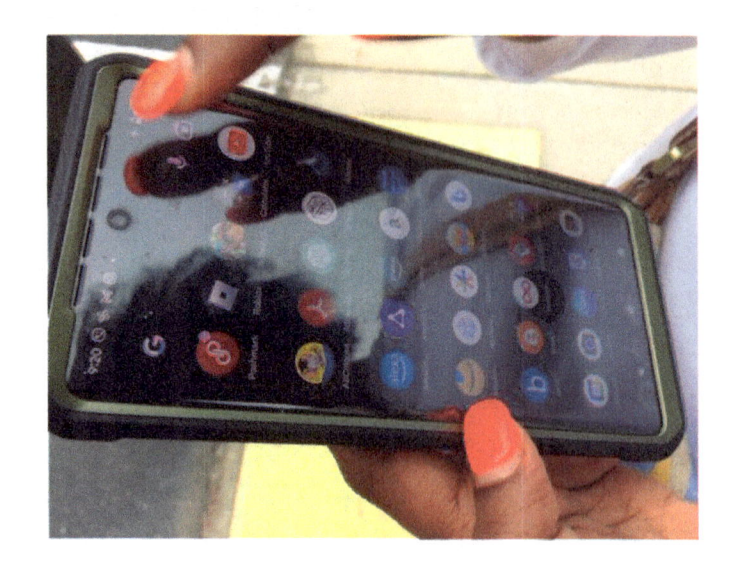

My God, I choose to remember not the former things, help me to delete all the hurts and negativity of my past, in Jesus name, Amen.(Isaiah 43:18-19)

PRUNING FLOWERS

My God, give me patience during my pruning season, so that I will bear more richer and finer fruit in Jesus name, Amen.(Jn 15:2)

REMOVING WEEDS

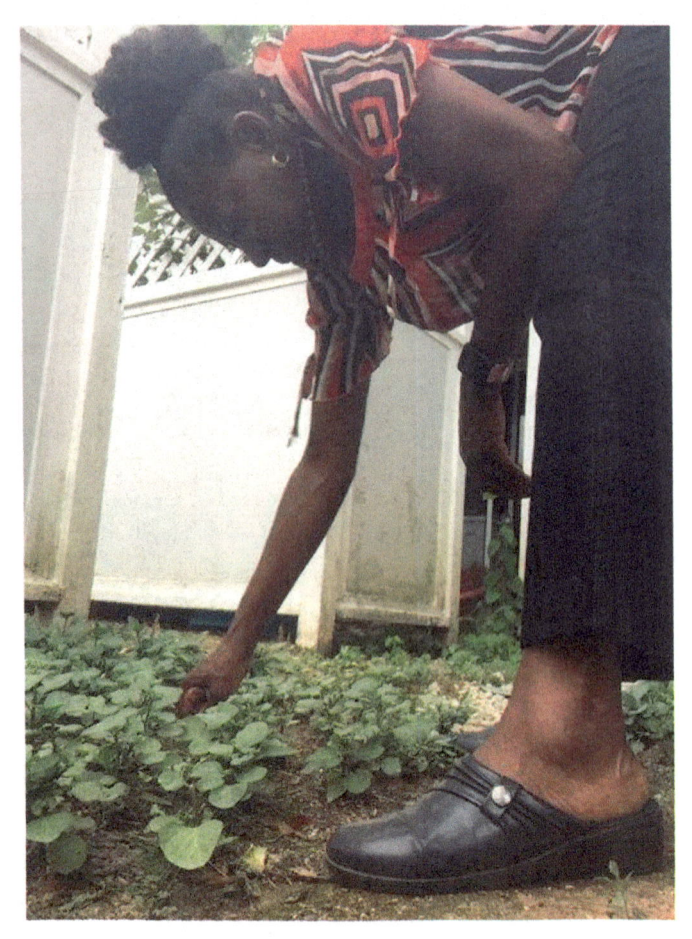

My God, please weed out the sin in my life which crowd out space for me to flourish in Jesus name, Amen.
(Col 3:10)

STARTING A CAR

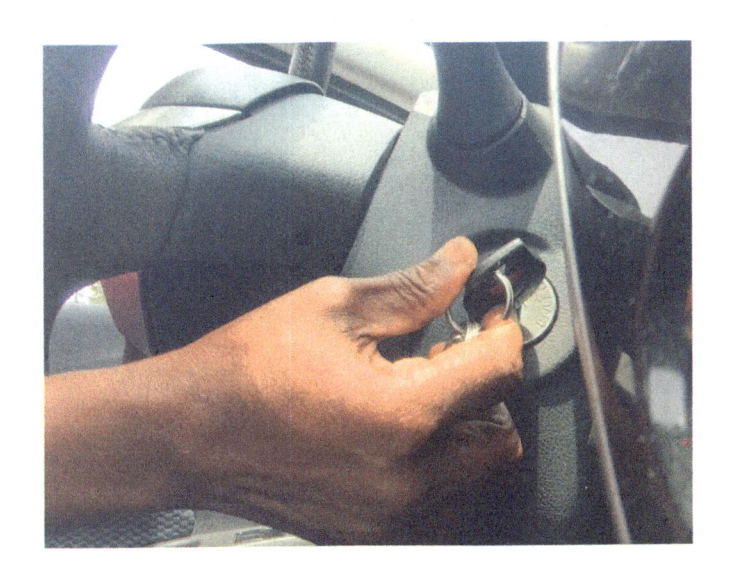

My God please activate the Holy Spirit in me, in Jesus name, Amen. (Eph 5:18)

OPENING WALLET

My God will fully supply my needs according to His riches in glory, Amen.(Phil 4:12)

WARMING FOOD IN THE MICROWAVE

My God, let me feel the warmth of your love, Amen.(Isaiah 41:10)

LEANING ON A WALL

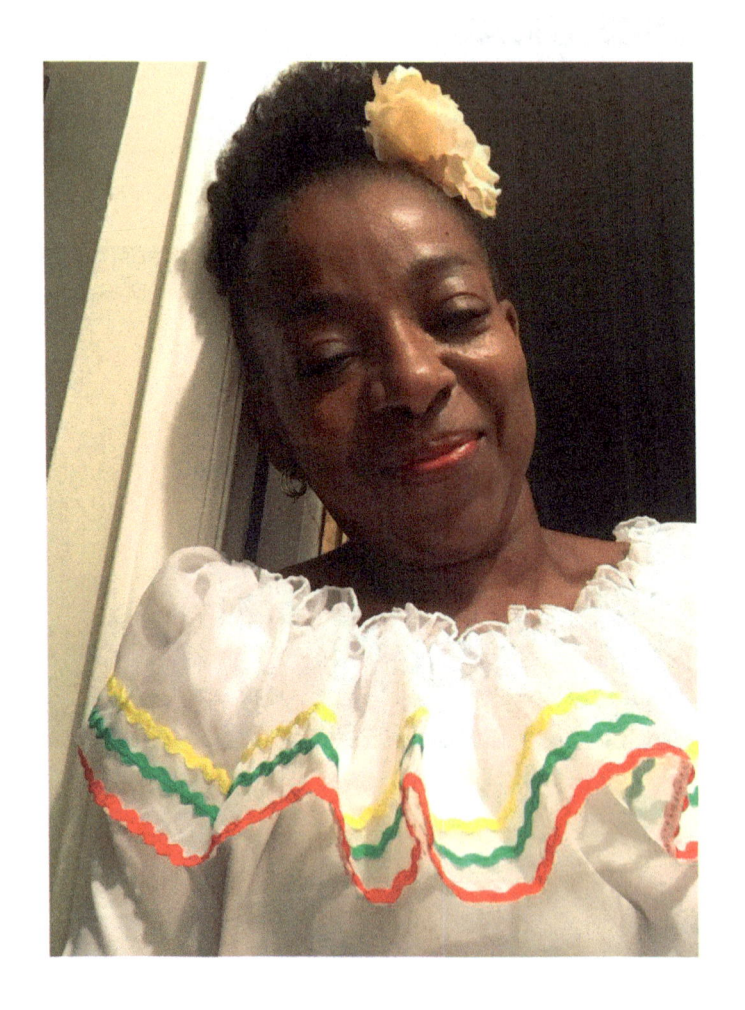

I lean on you Jesus for you are My Rock. (Ps 62:6)

PUTTING STUFF IN A BAG

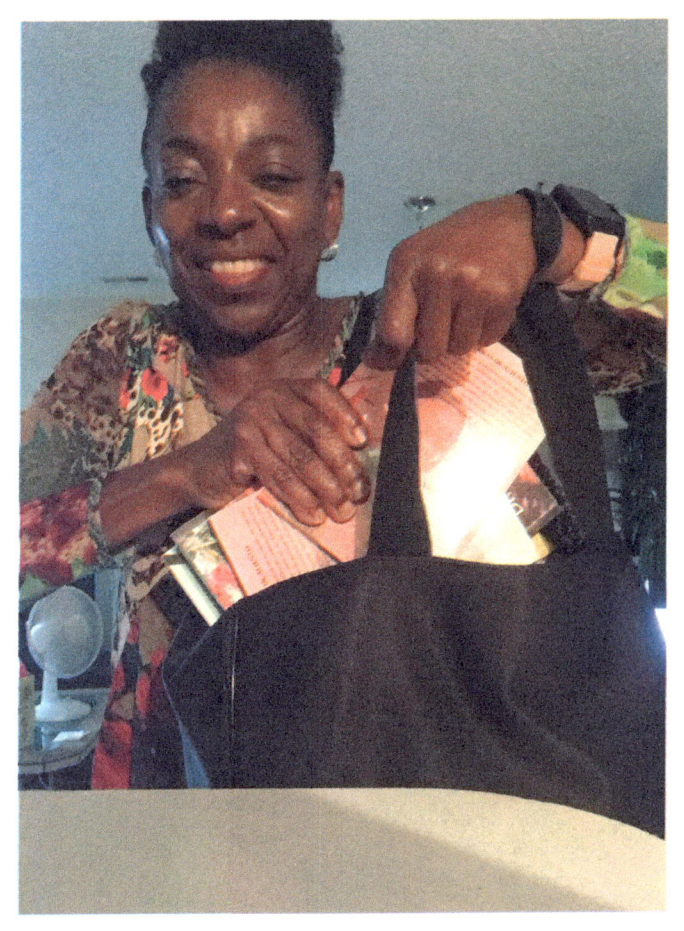

My God, I put all my trust in you, help me not to lean on my own understanding, Amen. (Prov 3:5-6)

SPRAYING AIR FRESHENER OR PERFUME

My God, may my sacrifice of praise be a sweet smelling aroma, acceptable and well pleasing to you, Amen.(Phil 4:18)

OPENING BLINDS/WINDOWS

Creator of heaven and earth, thank you for this new day and please open my eyes to see your beauty all around me, in Jesus name, Amen.(Ps 146:6)

CLIMBING A STEP

With you O Lord, I can do all things, for you give me the strength I need, Amen. (Phil 4:13)

SWIMMING

My God, with you on my side, I will stay afloat and the hard trials that come my way, will not drown me, Amen.(Isaiah 43:2)

PUTTING ON SEAT BELT

I will buckle up and put on the whole armor of God so I can stand against the wiles of the devil, Amen.(Eph 6:10-20)

EATING

My Lord, please feed me from the tree of life set in God's paradise, Amen. (Rev.2:7)

PUTTING SALT IN FOOD

My God, help me never to lose my saltiness in Jesus name, Amen.(Matt 5:13)

UNWRAPPING A CANDY

My God, please unlock the beauty that lies within me, in Jesus name, Amen. (1 Peter 3:4)

THE END

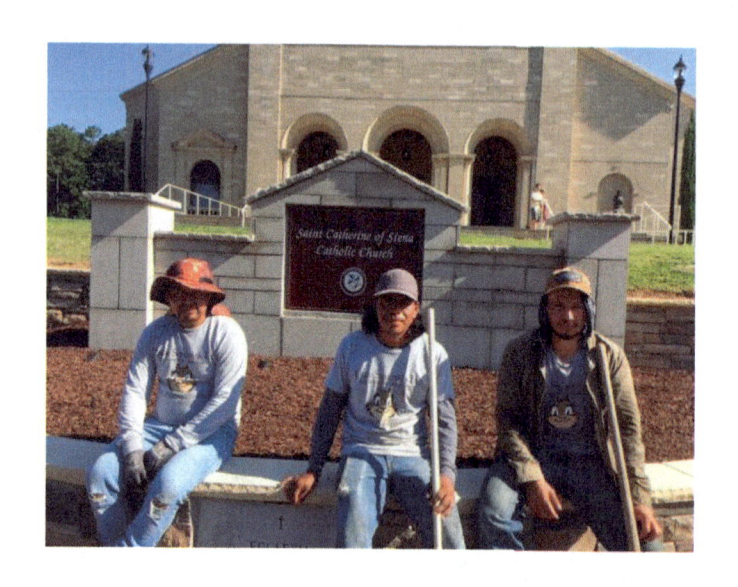

He that began a good work in you will surely bring it to completion, in Jesus name. Amen (Phil 1:6)

REFERENCE

An Attempt To Improve On Our Prayer Life Today by Rev. Fr. Pachomius Ebelubhuhi Okogie

OTHER BOOKS BY THE AUTHOR

Dr. Elizabeth Enoh is the author of "40 Days of Encouraging Words" and "Who Do You Say I Am?" available in Spanish and French. She has also compiled the following Inspirational Journals which have been translated into Spanish- "You Have Merit Peace:100 Days of Reflection","With Joy You Will Draw Water:100 Days of Reflection", "Heart Pondering:100 Days of Reflection", "Suffering With Grace:100 Days of Reflection", and "Love The Only Cure:100 Days of Reflection."

Made in the USA
Columbia, SC
17 August 2023